BiRTH
OF THE
COOL

HOW JAZZ GREAT MILES DAVIS
FOUND HIS SOUND

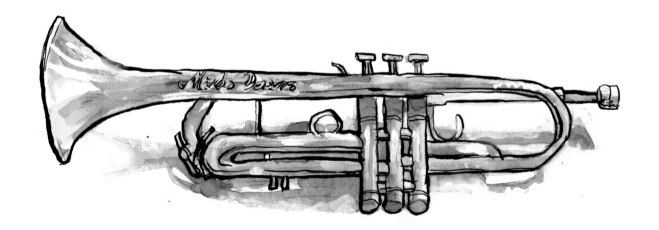

Kathleen Cornell Berman

illustrated by Keith Henry Brown

PAGE
STREET
KiDS

Mornings in East St. Louis,
Miles Davis
sits as close as he can get
to the radio.

Louis Armstrong's
soaring trumpet,
Duke Ellington's
sensational big band
dazzle Miles's imagination.

Swinging sounds of jazz
swirl together like
colors on a pinwheel.

Miles—
curious, smart,
crazy about music—
claps and sways,
lost in the moment
until his mom hollers,
"Time for school!"

Kids taunt and tease him,
just for being skinny, shy, and dark.
He plays baseball, swims,
and boxes like a champ.
But . . .
music means more.

When I got into music,
I went all the way into music;
I didn't have no time after
that for nothing else.

Blocks from home,
Miles watches riverboats
blow pillows of steam
while whistling, swishing
up the Mississippi River,
bringing musicians
from New Orleans
who play rollicking rhythms
in that Louis Armstrong way.
The perfect place for a boy
who loves music.

At night,
he lifts his window
to *listen* . . .
Melodies drift down the street.
Some croon country,
some cry the blues.
Sassy saxophones wail
through the night.

Miles can't sleep.
Taps his toes,
snaps his fingers,
can't stop thinking of ways
to make music of his own.

Summers—
Miles loves Grandpa's
Arkansas farm.
Different sounds echo,
the clip-clopping of his horse
beats rumbling rhythms
on dusty roads.
Miles imagines music . . .

Starry nights,
walking down winding roads,
the moon casts dark shadows
while guitars twang backwoods blues.
A woman's mournful voice sings
through tangled trees,
captivating him.

Saturday evening church,
soulful singing spills
into the night.
Miles *listens* . . .
Rhythmic clapping,
haunting harmonies
lift his spirits.
Sounds of Arkansas
stay with him
always.

Thirteenth birthday,
brand new gleaming trumpet!
Time for Miles to find his own sound.
Deep breaths, buzzed lips,
stuttering, squeaking,
sweaty brow, tight face.
He practices long tones
over and over and over.
Struggles to erase brassy notes
and create that round
sound he loves.

Treasured teacher,
Elwood Buchanan teaches Miles
the right way to play clearly.
Slaps his knuckles if
he shakes those notes.
He listens to the pro
who steers him on his path.

In high school band,
Mr. Buchanan pushes Miles
to play louder,
in his own style.
He comes through
with his best performance yet,
but prizes still go
to white kids.

Miles burns with humiliation.
Anger fuels his passion
to move forward,
to play harder,
to be undeniably
better than everyone else.
He blows those feelings
into something beautiful.

They play loud,
but I got the soul.

Miles plays dance music
while still in school,
makes money,
gains confidence,
dresses in style,
starts to improvise.
He carries his trumpet
everywhere.
Doesn't talk much,
but is always ready to play.

Bebop was about change,
about evolution. It wasn't
about standing still and
becoming safe.

Everybody's buzzing about
a new form of jazz.
Bebop—
far-out harmonies
with fast, flipping beats
that hop and bop.

Miles sets out,
trumpet in hand,
to hear the inventors of
this new style.
Miles is blown away
by the energy of the music.

Charlie "Bird" Parker's
blizzard of notes
explodes from the saxophone,
Dizzy Gillespie's
trumpet ripples melodies
like Miles has never heard before.
The band plays fast and free.

Then . . .
a dream come true.
A lucky break—
one of the bandmates
doesn't show up.
They ask Miles
to play.

The way that band was playing
music—that was all I wanted
to hear. It was something.

In awe,
he blows his trumpet.
Knees knocking,
can't hear himself,
too busy listening
to his idols.

Miles, not as ready
as he thought,
doesn't shine,
but bebop
flowers and flows
through his body.
Jazz
is all he wants to play.

Bird and Dizzy invite Miles
to look them up
in New York City.
Thrilled and ready,
he makes his plans.

I ain't never been scared of doing
new things, and I wasn't scared
when I got to New York City.

His father insists
he attend music school
in NYC.
Miles agrees,
but it's just a ploy to find
Bird and Dizzy.

He takes the train
to the city
where jazz thrives,
where his idols live,
where he can learn
to play his horn
like no other.

Miles wanders down
Fifty-Second Street—
"The Street"—
where jazz clubs
cram together,
jazz legends jam,
and music history is made.

Miles walks on air as
he *listens . . .*
Swinging sounds stream
from every doorway.

Mornings,
Juilliard School,
Miles studies classical music,
practices trumpet
between classes.

Nights,
he plays bebop
downtown,
uptown.
Gets a little sleep
before school starts.

Miles,
itching to play jazz
full-time,
wants to quit school,
to learn
from the best in the clubs.

Dad agrees
but warns his son:
Don't be like the mockingbird
that copies others.
Be your own man.
Be your own sound.

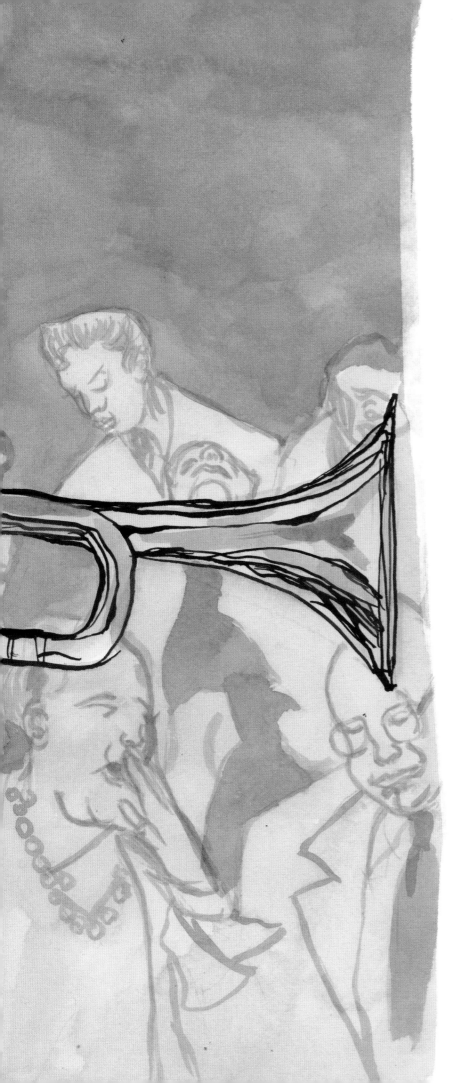

Dizzy leaves Bird's band—
Miles's big chance
to take his place.
He sounds like Dizzy,
but . . .
he can't play as high,
he can't play as fast.

I was impatient with myself
and most everything else.
But I kept it to myself
and kept my eyes and ears
wide open so that I could
keep on learning.

Miles hears music differently.
He doesn't like to play
a lot of notes.
He plays only
the important ones.
Some listeners put him down—
they want Dizzy's rippling trumpet.

He loses confidence,
wants to quit every night.
But Bird loves
his sound and
wants him to stay.
He tells Miles:
"Don't be afraid.
Go ahead and play."

Miles experiments
and discovers
a unique sound.
He crafts and perfects
his tone,
like a scientist of sound.
When he finds the right note,
he holds it
and savors it,
just for the beauty of it.

The way you change and help music is by trying to invent new ways to play.

Every night,
he *listens* . . .
and learns
from master musicians.
He also boxes to gain strength
and blowing power
to control his sound.
Overcome with exhaustion
yet feeling exhilarated,
he knows he's moving ahead,
away from bebop,
to create a new way
to play his trumpet.

Miles emerges
with confidence,
and a restlessness
he can't ignore.
Determined to try
something different,
he becomes leader
of his own group.
His chance to share
his music, his way.

Bird and Diz were ... fantastic,
challenging—but they weren't
sweet. Birth of the Cool was
different ... you could hear
everything and hum it also.

Miles searches for talented musicians
with modern ideas,
musicians that inspire him,
like Gil Evans.
They form a nonet,
a nine-piece band
that plays
slowly and mysteriously.

The band plays cool—
relaxed,
with a lighter,
lyrical feel.
Miles's playing punctuates
the new music with
poetic,
melancholy solos,
enchanting audiences,
and giving his voice
a chance to grow.

He performs with many
other groups
but loses focus,
can't find enough work,
encounters tough times.
His health declines.
People say
he's burnt out,
even though fans still listen
to his records.

He knows what he's got to do.
He climbs out
of his dark days
by playing his horn again.

Then, a chance meeting at a club.
Miles lines up
a surprise performance
at the prestigious
Newport Jazz Festival.
He is thrilled.
This is his chance
to restore
his faltering reputation.

He strolls onto the outdoor stage.
The crowd sits in silence.
He pushes his horn
into the microphone . . .

His sound pierces the air.
The audience feels a chill
as Miles plays his horn
like no other.

It was something else, man,
looking out at all those people
and then seeing them suddenly
standing up and applauding for
what I had done.

He wails the melody
with gripping emotion—
his mystical voice hangs
like a cloud,
leaving space
for each listener's
imagination to wander.

The band sizzles,
and Miles shines.
He's the star.
The audience goes wild,
stands on their feet,
electrified and satisfied
with the unforgettable
Miles Davis trumpet sound . . .

Like a human voice,
like the woman in Arkansas,
his horn sings, whispers,
and cries as his musical notes
become his words.
His trumpet is his voice.

Miles—
hip, cool,
stands as close
as he can get
and *listens* . . .
to what the others play,
thinking . . .
about what to change next.
With every step forward,
he breathes music.

A Note from Wynton Marsalis

By his mid-twenties, through his industry, intelligence, and creative insights, Miles Davis had invented a different way to play jazz on the trumpet. He was a master improviser who invented short, meaningful phrases. These phrases touch your heart in a very particular way. His improvised solos were logical, direct, honest, and deeply soulful. His playing was contagious. Miles was not afraid to let people know exactly how he felt.

Miles grew up in a time of stifling prejudice and racial segregation. He always did what he could to combat the ignorance and injustice of racial inequality that defined and ruined the quality of our national life. In his early twenties, he brought together an integrated group of young, talented musicians, arrangers, and composers. Their work together symbolized a movement toward social equality and democratic cooperation. It resulted in some recordings called *The Birth of the Cool*. It was exactly that: cool to come together, to be together, and to stay together.

Miles was deeply engaged with our American way of life. Through his music and his choices, he provoked and inspired us to see the world anew. He found new ways to express common songs and forms. His way of making music and of *being* fulfilled Duke Ellington's motto: "Be a number-one yourself and not a number-two somebody else." There was only *one* Miles Davis, and there will only ever be.

His music is diverse, interesting, and impactful. It expresses a wide range of styles, modes, and moods. Each recorded composition is supremely well crafted and unique. Miles paints with the most vivid colors. His music transports you to a world of ideas and emotions that will change your way of experiencing life—if you let it.

Kathleen Cornell Berman and Keith Henry Brown's story illuminates Miles Davis's early journey and purpose. It is just as direct, honest, and soulful as Miles's music . . . and it's fun to read and to see. Keith's pastels are as deeply felt as Miles's haunting sound. Kathleen's poetry is lyrical like Miles's lilting melodies. This book is an enjoyable and enriching way to teach and learn about one of our greatest artists and thinkers.

Author's Note

I first heard Miles Davis's music was when I was about ten years old. As my brother practiced his drums with Miles's records, I fell in love with Miles's trumpet sound. His music created a mood that I had never felt before. It was haunting and so different from the music I listened to. I became a lifelong fan of Miles Davis and jazz. As I wrote this book, I often listened to his music to inspire the words and rhythms of his story.

Miles's curiosity and desire to continually move forward was crucial to his success. This book recounts Miles's journey from ages 6 through 29. After playing with Charlie Parker and other groups, Miles declined an offer to join Duke Ellington's orchestra so that he could collaborate with Gil Evans and other musicians to create cool jazz, which had a brand-new feel in jazz music. The album *Birth of the Cool* is a compilation of the group's recorded sessions.

As Miles challenged himself, he changed music. He was at the forefront of developing cool jazz, modal jazz, hard bop, and fusion. Along with his trumpet playing, he was a composer, an arranger, and an outstanding bandleader. Miles brought out the best in his musicians. He gave them freedom to play their own ideas. He was a mentor to many well-known musical greats, such as John Coltrane, Bill Evans, Sonny Rollins, Herbie Hancock, Wayne Shorter, and others. He also formed relationships with rock musicians Jimi Hendrix and Prince. After Miles's performance at the 1955 Newport Jazz Festival, he continued to make jazz history with more albums. He was one of the most influential musicians of the twentieth century.

Once you hear Miles Davis's trumpet, you'll never forget it.

Illustrator's Note

The first time I heard what I later understood to be the "sound of jazz," it was from the horn of Miles Davis.

It began for me at the drop of a record needle and the first strain of "All Blues," a track on Miles Davis's groundbreaking album *Kind of Blue.* I was a music geek for most of my young life but never much delved into jazz, which seemed impossible to understand. But there was something about the flowing bass line and Miles's fluid trumpet on "All Blues" that drew me in. And it evoked the image of jazz, the *cool.*

Kind of Blue features five supremely gifted musicians in addition to Miles—tenor saxophonist John Coltrane, pianist Bill Evans (Wynton Kelly substitutes on one track), alto saxophonist Cannonball Adderley, bassist Paul Chambers, and drummer Jimmy Cobb—meshing their collective experience into something that was extraordinary and singular. In my mind's eye, I could see them in a half-lit studio, musicians smiling. I clung to this alluring world, and so began a lifelong love of this music.

But Miles himself was so much more. He was not just an entertainer; he was an artist, expressing himself through his instrument like a gifted painter (which he also was), creating strikingly beautiful sounds that were uniquely his own. Miles had a way of sharing his emotions through his art; very few of us can hear his sound without being moved in some way.

Finally, for me, Miles was simply a black man— someone who looked like *me.* He showed me that I could maybe someday be an artist too.

He helped me be me.

Selected Discography

Davis, Miles. *The Complete Birth of the Cool.* Recorded 1948–50. Capitol, 1998, compact disc.

———. *Kind of Blue.* Recorded 1959. Sony BMG Music Entertainment, 2008, compact disc.

———. *Young Miles.* Recorded 1945–50. Proper, 2001, 4 compact disc set.

Gillespie, Dizzy, and Charlie Parker. *Town Hall, New York City, June 22, 1945.* Recorded June 1945. Uptown Jazz, 2008, compact disc.

Parker, Charlie, and Miles Davis. *Bluebird: Legendary Savoy Sessions.* Recorded November 1945. Essential Jazz Classics, 2018, compact disc.

Bibliography

Carr, Ian. Miles Davis: *The Definitive Biography.* New York: Thunder's Mouth, 1998.

Chambers, J. K. Milestones: *The Music and Times of Miles Davis.* New York: Da Capo, 1998.

Crawford, Marc. "Miles Davis: Evil Genius of Jazz." *Ebony,* January 1961: 69–78.

Davis, Miles, and Quincy Troupe. *Miles, The Autobiography.* New York: Simon & Schuster, 1989.

Early, Gerald, ed. *Miles Davis and American Culture.* St. Louis: Missouri Historical Society, 2001.

Franckling, Ken. "Shining a Light on the Prince of Darkness." *JazzTimes,* August 1986.

Redmond, Eugene. "'So What' (?) . . . It's 'All Blues' Anyway: An Anecdotal/Jazzological Tour of Milesville." In *Miles Davis and American Culture,* edited by Gerald Early. St. Louis: Missouri Historical Society, 2001.

Rollins, Sonny, Bill Cosby, Herbie Hancock, Ron Carter, Clark Terry, Lenny White, Greg Tate, et al. *Miles Davis: The Complete Illustrated History.* Voyageur, 2012.

Szwed, John F. *So What: The Life of Miles Davis.* New York: Simon & Schuster, 2002.